# Broomstick Croch
# Fashions



BY

Margaret Helen Wilkes

W I BOOKS LTD
SEARCH PRESS LTD

# What is Broomstick Crochet?

Broomstick Crochet is a fascinating and unusual craft in which the wool is worked with a giant knitting needle, known as a Whizz Pin, and a crochet hook. The basic stitch pattern is easily learned, indeed beginners are always amazed at how quickly their work progresses. The attractive lacy pattern has the advantage of using less wool and it is ideal for a range of garments such as shawls, jumpers, waistcoats and cardigans.

As its name implies, this craft was originally worked using a broomstick handle, and it is sometimes known as Witchcraft Crochet for the same reason. Little is known about the history of this form of crochet. Although it is a relative novelty in Britain today, Broomstick Crochet is thought to have originated in this country, and to have been taken to America – where it is still popular – by the Pilgrim Fathers in the 1600s.

# Materials and equipment

**Pins**

Broomstick Crochet used to be worked using a broomstick handle, but nowadays you buy specially made needles known as Whizz Pins (or King Pins). These are usually made of plastic and are available in three sizes: 20 mm (40 cm long), 25 mm (40 cm long) and 25 mm (80 cm long). Only the 40-cm length pins are required for the patterns in this book, although the longer Pin can be used for any pattern specifying a 25-mm Pin. Whizz Pins are sold in craft shops.

**Crochet hooks**

The patterns in this book require crochet hooks in sizes 4.00, 5.00, 5.50, 6.00 and 7.00.

**Wools**

These patterns make use of a range of wools and yarns (e.g. aran, mohair, icelandic wool, mohair buffo and super match). It is important to use the wool specified for the best results.

**Abbreviations**

| | | | |
|---|---|---|---|
| alt | – alternate | mm | – millimetre |
| beg | – beginning | patt(s) | – pattern(s) |
| ch | – chain | rep | – repeat |
| cm | – centimetre | rnd | – round |
| dc | – double crochet | sp | – space |
| dec | – decrease | ss | – slip stitch |
| gr | – group | st(s) | – stitch(es) |
| in | – inch | tog | together |
| inc | – increase | tr | – treble |
| lp(s) | – loop(s) | | |

**Enlarging and reducing sizes**

Based on the stitch tension i.e. 1 patt 2½ cm (1 inch). The width of the basic garment can be adjusted up or down by adding or subtracting patts for every centimetre/inch difference required. The length may also be adjusted by adding or subtracting patts for every centimetre/inch difference required.

When working with fewer or additional stitches, provision must be made for these at the armhole, shoulder and neck shaping.

A difference in patterns should be calculated on each of the armholes i.e. 1 patt, 2½ cm (1 inch).

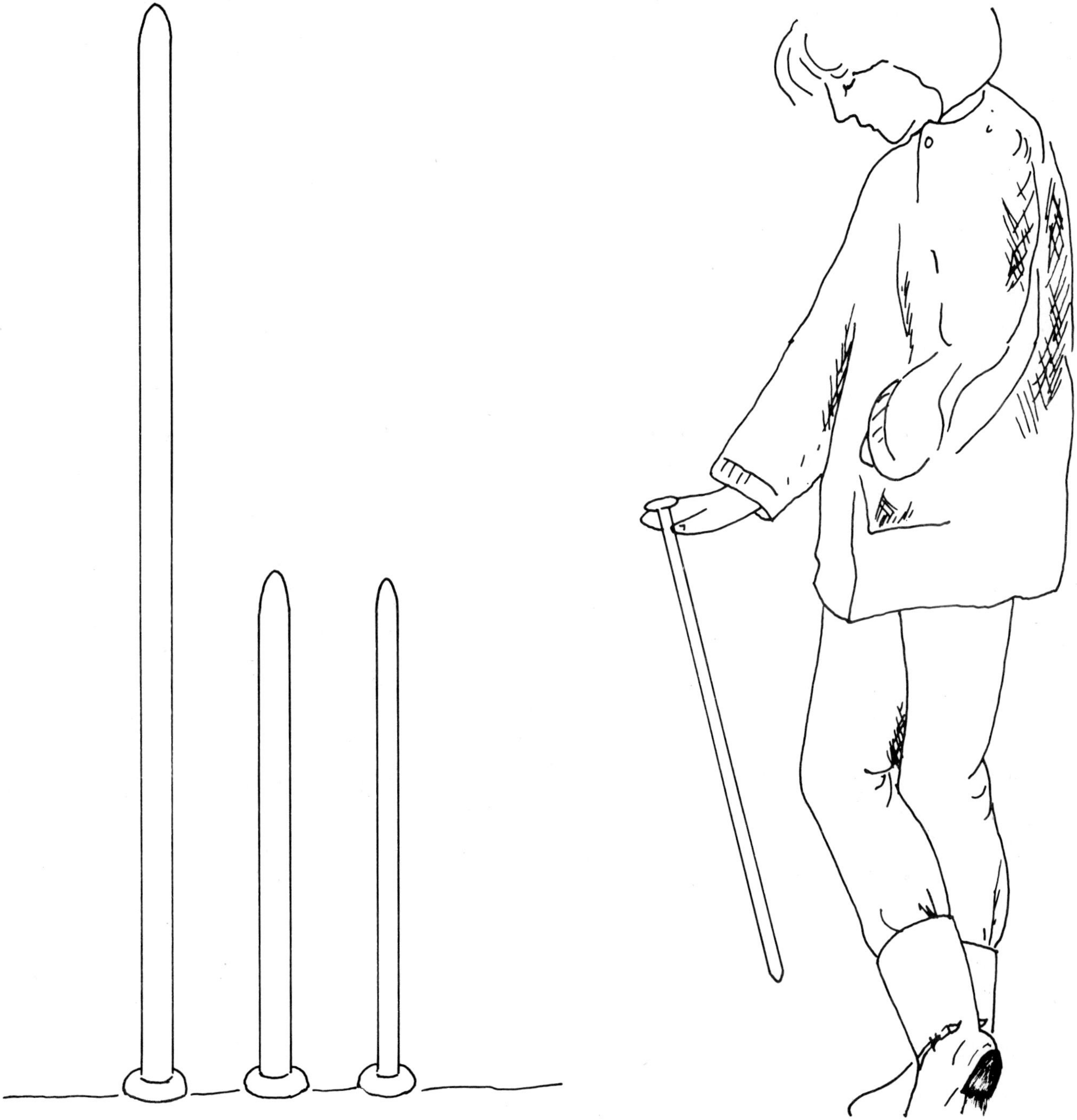

# Broomstick Crochet step-by-step

These diagrams give step-by-step instructions for the basic Broomstick Crochet pattern. Beginners should practise this basic pattern by starting with 20 chain (Step 1) to make 4 patterns with 4 loops.

1 Crochet the chain loosely.
2 Fix the Whizz Pin firmly between your knees or between your thigh and the arm of your chair. Lift the first chain stitch on to the Whizz Pin.
3 Insert the crochet hook through the next chain stitch, wool over the hook, draw through the stitch.
4 Place this loop over the Whizz Pin. Repeat from Step 3 with the next chain stitch and continue to the end of the row.
5 Take off 5 loops together.*
6 Hold the loops together.
7 Draw the wool through the loops with the crochet hook.
8 Make 1 chain stitch.
9 Work 5 double crochet.
10 Work 5 double crochet in the next 5 loops together (i.e. repeat Steps 5–9). Continue to the end of the row.
11 Draw a loop through each double crochet stitch and place it on to the Whizz Pin.

The last 2 rows form the pattern.

* Note. Some articles are made with fewer or more loops taken off together.

**Samples**
The basic stitch pattern shown in the step-by-step diagrams can be varied to create different effects. At the beginning of each pattern in this book, are instructions for making a small sample swatch showing the stitch variations used for that pattern. This allows you to practise the variation and check your tension before you start on the garment itself.

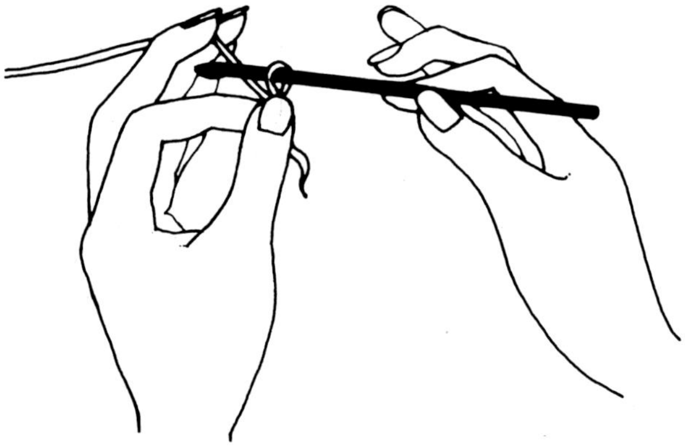

**1** Make 20 chains, loosely.

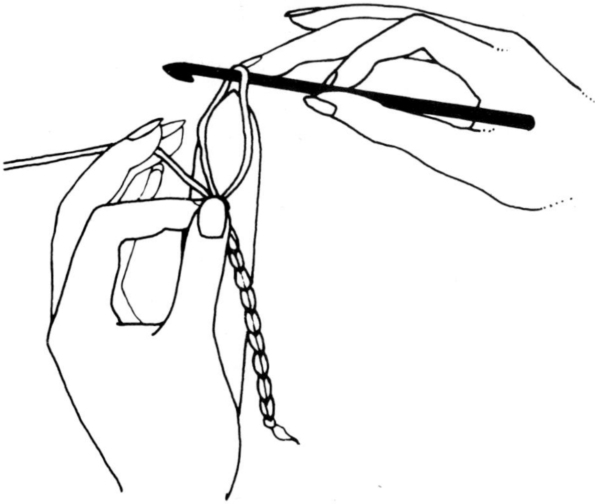

2 Fix the Whizz Pin firmly between the knees or in other rigid position, and place the first chain (i.e. the last one to be made) on to the Whizz Pin.

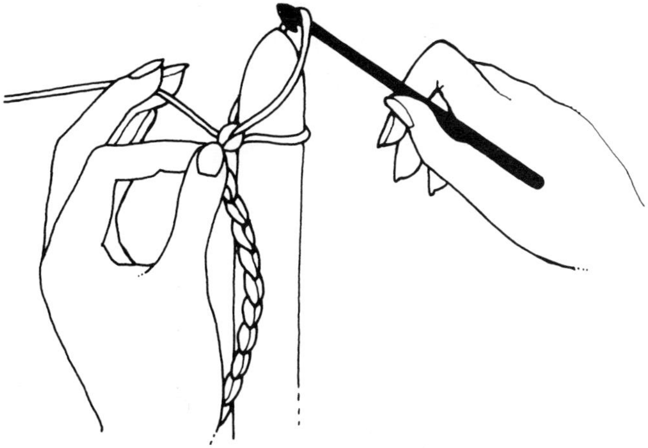

4 Place this new loop over the Whizz Pin and continue to do this (3 and 4) till the end of the chain. Now turn the chain round to the right-hand side of the Whizz Pin as shown.

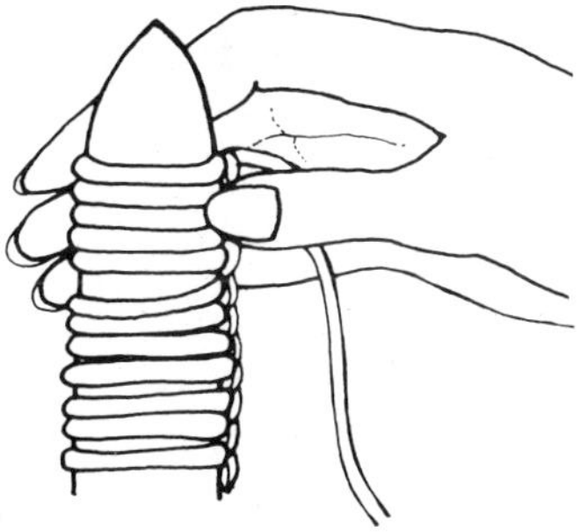

5 Slip 5 loops off the Whizz Pin together.

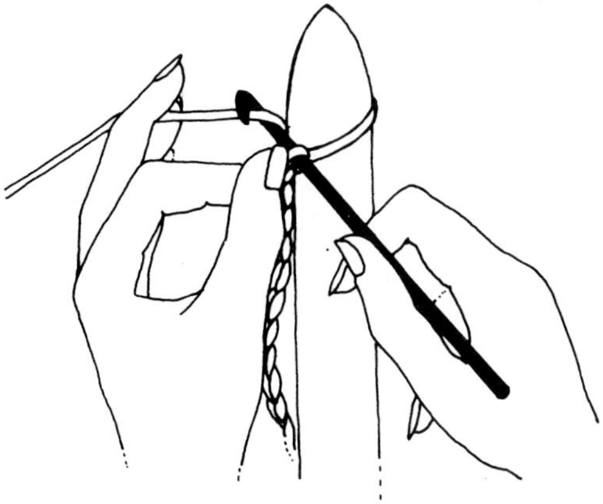

3 Place the hook through the next chain st., yarn over hook, and pull through.

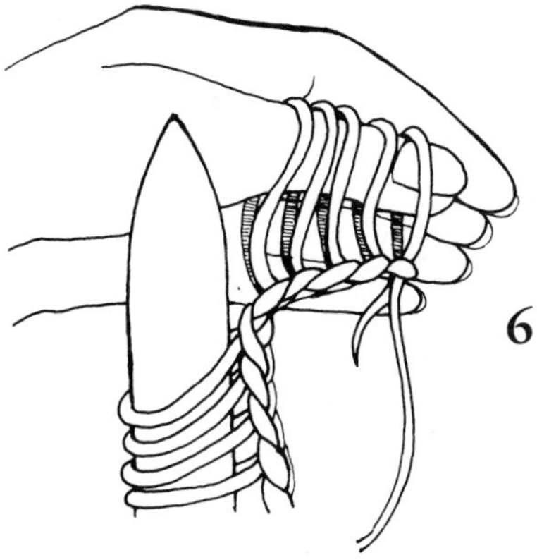

6 Hold them together as one loop. (The hook may be entered into either end of the loops, but do it in the same way throughout, as this will decide the direction in which the loops cross over.)

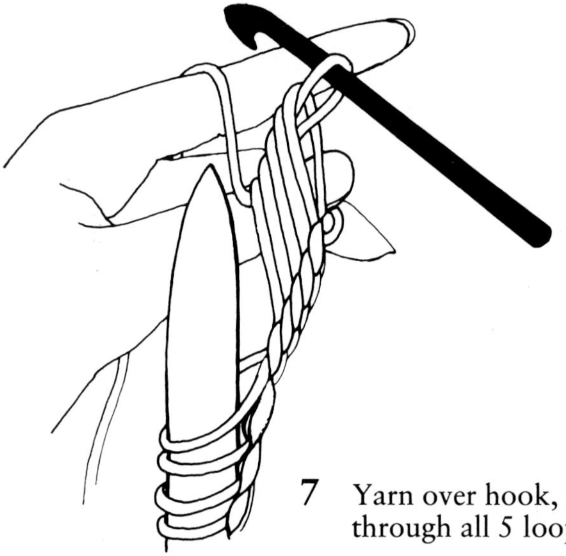

**7** Yarn over hook, and pull through all 5 loops.

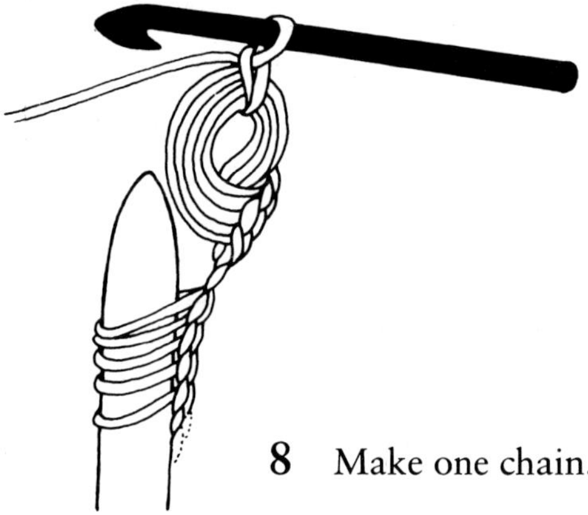

**8** Make one chain.

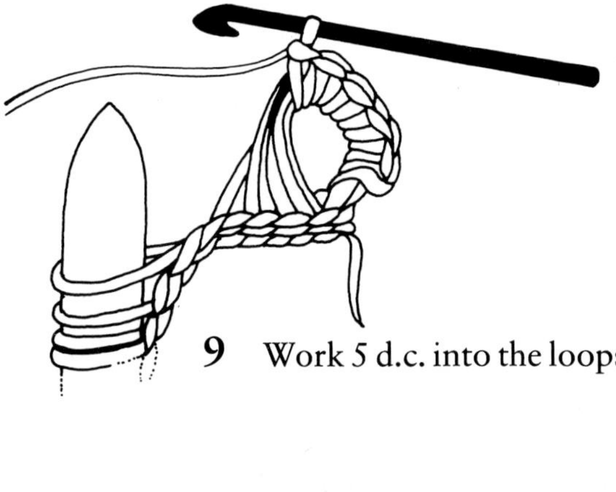

**9** Work 5 d.c. into the loops.

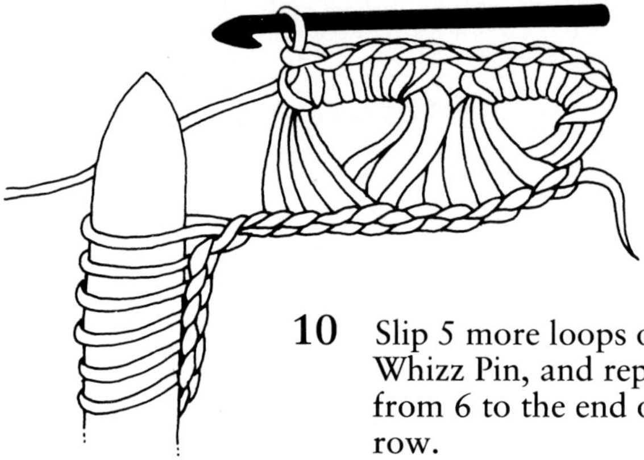

**10** Slip 5 more loops off the Whizz Pin, and repeat from 6 to the end of the row.

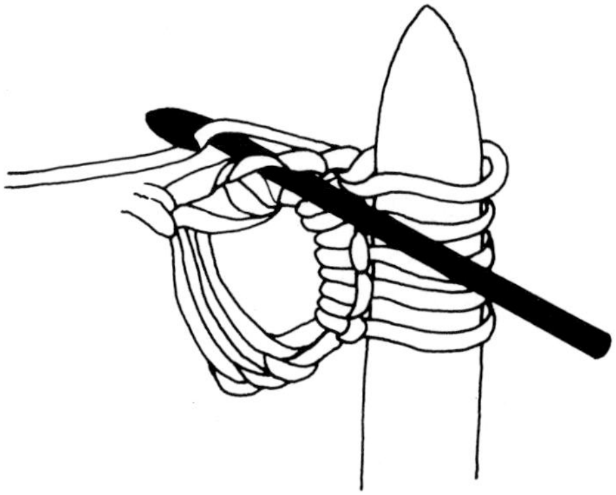

**11** Make a new set of loops by hooking the yarn through each d.c. st. and placing it on the Whizz Pin as in 4. Now continue as in 5. These 2 rows form the pattern.

*Mohair top*

**Sleeves**
With 6.00 hook make 65 ch.
Row 1: 1 dc into 2nd ch from hook, 1 dc into each ch, to end of row. (64 dc).
Row 2: Draw through 64 lps.
Row 3: 4 dc into 4 lps tog, rep to end of row. (16 patts across).
Rep last 2 rows until 16 patts length have been worked from beg. Fasten off.

**Making up:**
Sew shoulders tog 7 patts each side, leaving 7 patts front and back for neck. Sew side seams from bottom edge leaving 8 patts back and front for armholes. Sew sleeve, ch edge to top edge, match each patt front and back of armhole, the side seams.

**Border:**
Bottom edge of sweater, with 5.00 hook, right side of work, join 1 ch 1 dc into same st *(miss 1 ch. 1 dc into next ch st) rep from * to end of rnd, join with a ss.

Rnd 1: 2 ch 1 hlf tr into each dc to end of rnd, join with a ss. Turn.
Rnd 2: 2 ch 1 hlf tr into each hlf tr to end of rnd, join with a ss. Turn.
Rep last rnd 5 times more. Fasten off.

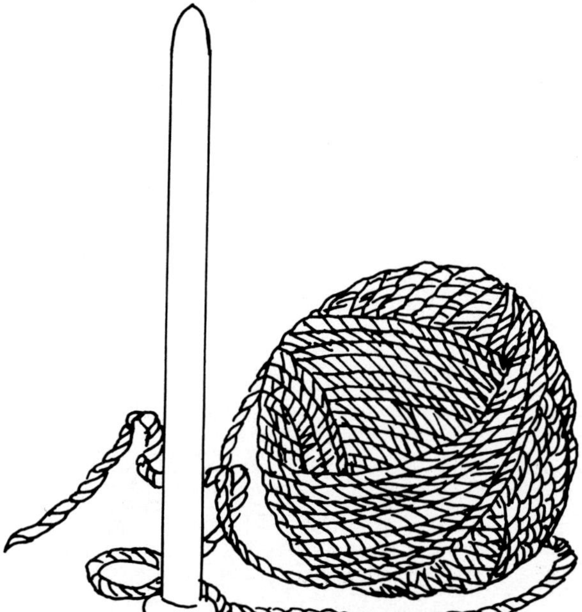

# Falkland sweater

**Sample**
With 20 mm Whizz Pin and 6.00 hook make 21 ch. (See pp. 4–5).
Row 1: Miss 1 ch 1 dc into each ch (20 dc).
Row 2: Draw through 20 lps on to Whizz Pin.
Row 3: 4 dc into 4 lps tog. Rep to end of row.
Last 2 rows form patt.

**Size:** Bust 86/91 cm (34/36 in). Length of sleeve 41 cm (16 in). Length from back of neck 58 cm (23 in).

**Tension:** 3 patts – 8 cm (3 in) across.

**Materials:** 15 (50 grm) balls Falkland Island Wool. 1 20 mm (¾ in) Whizz Pin.
5.00 and 6.00 crochet hooks.

**Front and back alike:** (Note: Use 5.00 hook to draw lps through). With 6.00 hook make 85 ch.
Row 1: 1 dc into 2nd ch from hook, 1 dc into each ch st, to end of row. (84 dc).
Row 2: Draw through 84 lps.
Row 3: 4 dc into 4 lps tog, rep to end of row. (21 patts across).
Rep last 2 rows until 19 patts length have been worked from beg Fasten off.

*Falkland sweater*

*Aran waistcoat*

Row 3: Join contrast with 5.00 hook 2 ch 1 tr into 1st front lp of dc. Rep 1 tr into front dc to end of row. Fasten off.
Row 4: Join main colour with 6.00 hook 1 ch 1 dc into 1st tr 1 dc into each tr.
Rep. to end of row.
Row 5: Draw through 26 lps.
Row 6: 4 dc into 4 lps tog. Rep to last 6 lps 4 dc into 6 lps tog.
Row 7: As row 3.
Row 8: As row 4.
Row 9: Draw through 24 lps.
Row 10: As row 2.
Row 11: As row 3.
Row 12: As row 4.
Row 13: Draw through 22 lps.
Row 14: As row 6.
Row 15: As row 3.
Row 16: As row 4. Fasten off.

**Right front:**
Wrong side join wool at armhole 28th dc from front edge. Draw through 28 lps.
(7 patts across). Work as left front reversing the decreases.

**Back:**
Wrong side work across 14 patts leaving 2 patts each side for armholes work patt (length) 4 times. Fasten off.
Sew shoulders tog.

**Border:** Front edge and armholes.
Row 1: Join main colour, 6.00 hook at right front corner 6 dc across each patt to shoulder. Fasten off.
Row 2: Right front: Join at right corner 1 dc into back lp of each dc to shoulder. Fasten off.

**Left front:**
Join at shoulder, work as right front.
Armholes: Work border as front leaving 2 patts underarm.

Row 3: Draw through 34 lps.
Row 4: 4 dc into 6 lps tog * (4 dc into 4 lps tog) rep from * to end of row.
Row 5: Draw through 32 lps.
Row 6: As row 2.
Row 7: Draw through 30 lps.
Row 8: As row 4.
Row 9: Draw through 28 lps.
Row 10: As row 2.
Row 11: Draw through 26 lps.
Row 12: As row 4.
Row 13: Draw through 24 lps.
Row 14: As row 2.
Row 15: Draw through 22 lps.
Row 16: As row 4. Fasten off.

Join to centre to beg of 9th patt.

Row 1: Draw through 36 lps.
Row 2: *(4 dc into 4 lps tog) rep from * to last 4 lps. 2 dc into 4 lps tog. Turn.
Row 3: Draw through 34 lps.
Row 4: *(4 dc into 4 lps tog) rep from * to last 6 lps. 4 dc into 6 lps tog.
Row 5: Draw through 32 lps.
Row 6: As row 2.
Row 7: Draw through 30 lps.
Row 8: As row 4.
Row 9: Draw through 28 lps.
Row 10: As row 2.
Row 11: Draw through 26 lps.
Row 12: As row 4.
Row 13: Draw through 24 lps.
Row 14: As row 2.
Row 15: Draw through 22 lps.
Row 16: As row 4. Fasten off.

Sew shoulders tog. (5 patts across each side).

**Sleeves:** Front of armhole, right side, 7 patts from shoulder, join yarn, 1 ch, *(4 dc into each patt) rep from * to back of armhole (56 dc). Turn.
Row 1: Draw through 56 lps.
Row 2: 4 dc into 4 lps tog, rep to end of row. (14 patts across). Rep last 2 rows until 16 patts length have been worked, last row ending (3 dc into 4 lps tog). Fasten off.

**Making up:** Sew side and sleeve seams tog.

**Border:** With 4.00 hook, join at bottom edge, 1 ch, *(1 dc into each ch st 3 times, miss 1 ch) rep from * to end of row (108 dc).
Next rnd: 1 dc into each dc. Work 6 more rnds. Fasten off.

**Sleeves:** Join yarn 1 ch. *(2 dc miss 1 dc) rep from * to end of rnd. (28 dc).
Next rnd: 1 dc into each dc. Work 6 more rnds. Fasten off.

**Neck:** Join at left shoulder *(4 dc into each patt) rep from * left side, right side and back (2 dc into centre of V neck).
Rnd 1: left side, 1 dc into each dc to 2 centre dc, (dec, by placing hook into 1st dc, yarn over hook and draw through, hook through next dc, yarn over hook, and draw through, yarn over hook, draw through 3 lps on hook). 1 dc into each dc right side and back.
Rnd 2: 1 dc into each dc to centre dc (dec by missing centre dc) 1 dc into each dc right side and back.
Rep last 2 rnds twice more. Fasten off.

# Aran waistcoat

**Sample**
With main colour and 6.00 hook make 17 ch. (See pp. 4–5).
Row 1: With 5.00 hook miss 1 ch, 1 dc into each ch st. (16 dc).
Row 2: Draw through 16 lps.
Row 3: With 6.00 hook 4 dc into 4 lps tog. Rep to end of row (4 patts across).
Row 4: Join contrast with 5.00 hook, 2 ch 1 tr into 1st front lp of dc. Rep 1 tr into front of each dc to end of row. Fasten off.
Row 5: Join main colour with 6.00 hook, 1 ch 1 dc into 1st dc, Rep 1 dc into each dc to end of row.
Last 4 rows form patt.

**Size:** Chest 81/86 cm (32/34 in). Length from back of neck 61 cm (24 in).

**Tension:** 1 patt 6 cm (2¼in) length.

**Materials:** Main colour 5 (50 grm) balls Lister Lee, 3 balls contrast. 25 mm (1 in) Whizz Pin. 5.00 and 6.00 crochet hooks.

**Worked all-in-one:** With main colour and 6.00 hook make 129 ch.
Row 1: Right side of work. With 5.00 hook miss 1 ch 1 dc into each ch to end of row.
Row 2: Draw through 128 lps.
Row 3: With 6.00 hook 4 dc into 4 lps tog. Rep to end of row. Fasten off.
Row 4: Join contrast with 5.00 hook, 2 ch 1 tr into 1st front lp of dc. Rep 1 tr into front of each dc to end of row. Fasten off.
Row 5: Join main colour with 6.00 hook, 1 ch 1 dc into 1st dc. Rep 1 dc into each dc to end of row.
Last 4 rows form patt. Rep patt 6 times more.
**Left front:** Shape neck.
Row 1: Draw through 28 lps (7 patts across). Turn.
Row 2: Shape front. 4 dc into 4 lps tog. Rep to last 4 lps 2 dc into 4 lps tog.
Fasten off.

# Mohair cardigan

**Sample**
With 25 mm Whizz Pin and 7.00 hooks, make 20 ch. (See pp. 4–5).
Row 1: Draw lps through ch sts on to Whizz Pin. (20 lps).
Row 2: 5 dc into 5 lps tog. Rep to end of row.
Row 3: Draw through 20 lps.
Row 4: 5 dc into 5 lps tog.
Last 2 rows form patt.

**Size:** 87/92 cm (34/36 in). Length from back of neck 65 cm (25½ in).

**Sleeve:** Length 46 cm (18 in).

**Tension:** 2 patts. 7½ cm (3 in) length.

**Materials:** 15 (25 grm) balls Lister Tahiti. 1 25 mm (1 in) Whizz Pin. 5.50 and 7.00 crochet hooks.

**Back:** And back of sleeves worked all-in-one. Work Broomstick patt with 7.00 hook make 180 ch.
Row 1: Draw through 180 lps.
Row 2: Right side, 5 dc in 5 lps. tog. Rep to end of row (36 patts across).
Rep last 2 rows until (5 patts length) have been worked. Fasten off.
Centre back: Wrong side. Join yarn to 13th patt across.
Row 1: Draw through 60 lps. (12 patts across).
Row 2: 6 dc in 5 lps tog. Rep to end of row.
Row 3: Draw through 72 lps.
Row 4: 6 dc in 6 lps tog. Rep to end of row.
Rep last 2 rows 10 times more (17 patts length) from back of neck. Fasten off.

*Mohair cardigan*

*Super match blouse*

**Left front and sleeve:**
Make 75 ch.
Row 1: Draw through 75 lps.
Row 2: 5 dc in 5 lps tog. Rep to end of row (15 patts across).
Row 3: Draw through 75 lps.
Row 4: Front shaping 8 dc in the first 5 lps. *(5 dc in 5 lps tog). Rep from * to end of row.
Row 5: Draw through 78 lps.
Row 6: 5 dc in 3 lps tog * (5 dc in 5 lps tog). Rep from * to end of row.
Row 7: Draw through 80 lps.
Row 8: As row 4.
Row 9: Draw through 83 lps.
Row 10: As row 6. Fasten off. (sleeve).

Front: Wrong side join to 13th patt across (leaving 12 patts sleeve).
Row 1: Draw through 25 lps.
Row 2: 6 dc in 5 lps tog. Rep to end of row.
Row 3: Draw through 30 lps.
Row 4: 6 dc in 6 lps tog. Rep to end of row.
Rep last 2 rows 10 times more.

**Right front and sleeve:**
Make 75 ch.
Row 1: Draw through 75 lps.
Row 2: 5 dc in 5 lps tog. Rep to end of row (15 patts across).
Row 3: Draw through 75 lps.
Row 4: *(5 dc in 5 lps tog) Rep from * to last 5 lps. 8 dc in 5 lps tog.
Row 5: Draw through 78 lps.
Row 6: *(5 dc in 5 lps tog) Rep from * to last 3 lps. 5 dc in 3 lps tog.
Row 7: Draw through 80 lps.
Row 8: As row 4.
Row 9: Draw through 83 lps.
Row 10: As row 6.

**Front:**
Row 11: Draw through 25 lps leaving (12 patts sleeve).
Row 12: 6 dc in 5 lps tog. Rep to end of row.
Row 13: Draw through 30 lps.
Row 14: 6 dc in 6 lps tog. Rep to end of row.
Rep last 2 rows 10 times more. Fasten off.

**Making up:**
**Left front and sleeve:** Place to back wrong side, sew side seam and bottom edge of sleeve tog.

**Right side:** Fold over front and sleeve, crochet top part of sleeve and shoulder tog match patt, starting at sleeve.
Row 1: 5.50 hook join yarn, hook through front and back st with a ss 1 dc in the same st work 5 dc in front and back patt tog. Rep to neck, turn.
Row 2: 7.00 hook * (1 tr in lst dc 1 ss in next dc) Rep from * to end of sleeve. Fasten off.

**Right front and sleeve:** Work the same as left front, starting at neck.

**Sleeve borders:**
Rnd 1: 4 dc in each patt to end of rnd join with a ss. Turn.
Rnd 2: *(1 tr in lst dc 1 ss in next dc) Rep from * to end of rnd ss to join. Fasten off.

**Front and neck border:** Broomstick Patt.
Right side join to corner, right front 5 dc in each patt. Rep across back of neck to corner left front. Turn.
Row 1: Draw through 200 lps.
Row 2: 5 dc in 5 lps tog. Rep to end of row.
Rep last 2 rows 3 times more. Fasten off.

**Front bottom edge:** of Broomstick patt (5 dc in each patt 4 times). Fasten off.

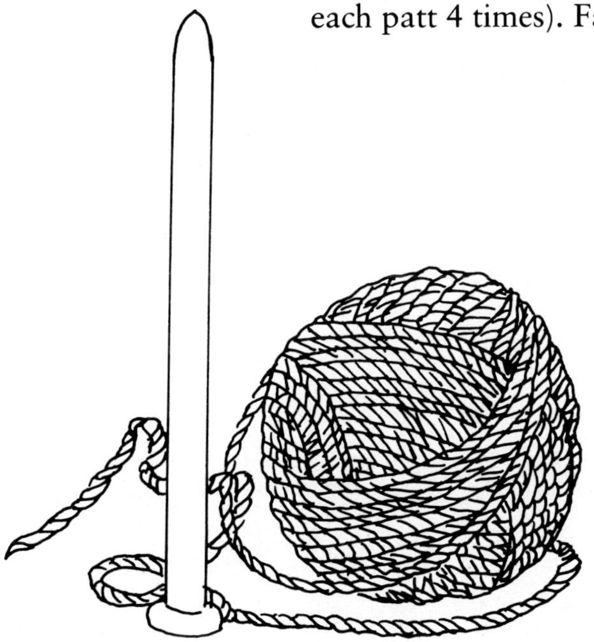

# Super match blouse

**Sample**
Note: dec row is right side of work.
With 20 mm Whizz Pin and 5.00 hook, make 20 ch. (See pp. 4–5).
Row 1: Draw lps through ch sts on to Whizz Pin. (20 lps).
Row 2: 5 dc into 5 lps tog. Rep to end of row. (4 patts across).
Row 3: Draw through 20 lps.
Row 4: As row 2.
Last 2 rows form patt.

**Size:** Bust 81/86 cm (32/34 in). Length from shoulder 56 cm (22 in).

**Tension:** 2 patts – 5 cm (2 in) across.

**Materials:** 10 (25 grm) balls Emu Super match. 1 20 mm (¾ in) Whizz Pin. 4.00, 5.00 and 5.50 crochet hooks.

Note: dec row is right side of work.

**Back and front alike:**
**Right Shoulder:** With 5.00 hook make 25 ch.
Row 1: Draw lps through each st. (25 lps).
Row 2: 5 dc into 5 lps tog. Rep to end of row. (5 patts across).
Row 3: Draw through 25 lps.
Row 4: As row 2. Last 2 rows form patt.
Rep patt once more, ending dc row (3 patts length) continue to make 35 ch for neck, do not break yarn.

**Left shoulder:** Work as right shoulder, omit last dc row, break yarn, join ch to lps. 5 dc into 5 lps tog. Rep to end of row.

*Blue mohair jacket*

Row 1: Draw through 25 lps, then into each ch st 35 times, then 25 lps. (85 lps).
Row 2: 5 dc into 5 lps tog. rep to end of row. (17 patts across).
Row 3: Draw through 85 lps.
Row 4: As row 2.
Rep. last 2 rows until (18 patts length) have been worked from shoulder.

**Waist:** With 4.00 hook 2 ch 1 tr into same st *(1 tr into each dc) rep from * to end of row (85 tr).
Next row: 1 ch * (1 dc into each tr) rep from * to end of row (85 dc).
Row 1: Draw through 85 lps.
Row 2: 5.50 hook 5 dc into 5 lps tog. Rep to end of row.
Rep last 2 rows until 5 patts length from waist have been worked.
Next row: Draw through 85 lps.

**Edge:** (3 dc. 2 ch. 3 dc) into 5 lps tog. Rep to end of row. Fasten off.
Sew shoulders tog.

**Sleeves:** Work right side from armholes, with 5.00 hook, join to 8 patts from shoulder 40 dc from shoulder 40 dc. (80 dc) 16 patts across). Turn.
Row 1: Draw through 80 lps.
Row 2: 5 dc into 5 lps tog 6 times, 10 dc into 5 lps tog 4 times, 5 dc into 5 lps tog 6 times.
Row 3: Draw through 100 lps.
Row 4: 5 dc into 5 lps tog. Rep to end of row.
Rep last 2 rows until 7 patts length have been worked.
Next row: Draw through 100 lps.

**Edge:**
Row 1: With 4.00 hook, *(3 dc into 5 lps tog, 2 dc into next 5 lps tog). Rep from * to end of row (50 dc).
Row 2: 2 ch, 1 tr into same st *(1 tr into each dc) rep from * to end of row (50 tr).
Row 3: 1 ch * (1 dc into each tr) rep from * to end of row (50 dc).
Row 4: Draw through 50 lps.
Row 5: With 5.00 hook 5 dc into 5 lps tog, rep to end of row.
Row 6: Draw through lps.
Row 7: (3 dc 2 ch 3 dc) into 5 lps tog. Rep to end of row. Fasten off.

**Making up:**
Sew side and sleeve seams tog.
Neck Edge: Front and Back alike.
Front with 5.00 hook, join at shoulder 5 dc into each patt, 3 times to ch 35 dc into each ch st, then 5 dc into each patt to shoulder, 65 dc.
Row 1: Draw through 65 lps.
Row 2: (2 dc 2 ch 2 dc) into 5 lps tog, rep to end of row. Fasten off.
Back as Front.
Sew tog patts on dc row, each side.

# Blue mohair jacket

**Sample**
With 1 20 mm Whizz Pin. 7.00 crochet hook.
Note: Work dc, loosely throughout except for borders. For best results when working with mohair buffo yarn gently allow the coloured plumes to flow out onto right side of work as the crochet proceeds. Broomstick pattern is worked with 2 lps tog.
Make 12 ch loosely.
Row 1: Draw lps through ch st (12 lps).
Row 2: Wrong side of work, 1 ch 2 dc in 2 lps tog *(2 dc in 2 lps tog) rep from * to end of row.
Row 3: Draw lps through each dc.
Row 4: As row 2.
Last 2 rows form patt.

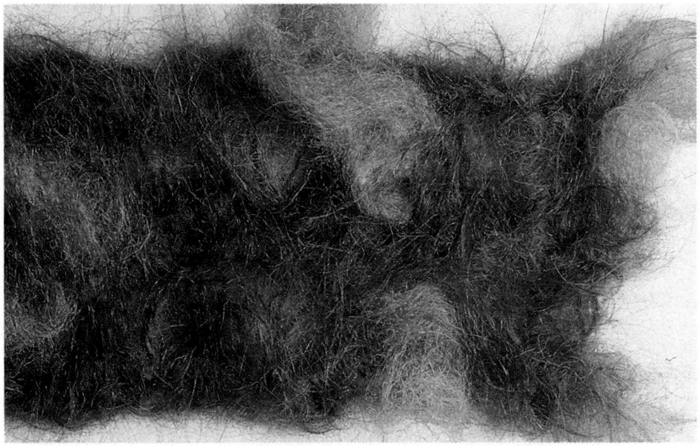

**Size:** 91/102 cm. 36/40 in.

**Tension:** 2 patts – 5 cm (2 in) across.

**Materials:** Filatura Di Crosa quality mohair buffo. 5 (50 grm) balls. 1 20 mm Whizz Pin. 7.00 crochet hook.

Note: Work dc, loosely throughout except for borders. For best results when working with mohair buffo yarn gently allow the coloured plumes to flow out onto right side of work as the crochet proceeds. Broomstick pattern is worked with 2 lps tog.
Make 118 ch loosely.
Row 1: Draw lps through each ch st (118 lps).
Row 2: Wrong side of work, 1 ch 2 dc in 2 lps tog *(2 dc in 2 lps tog) rep from * to end of row.
Row 3: Draw lps through each dc.
Row 4: As row 2.
Last 2 rows form patt.
Rep last 2 rows until 8 patts length have been worked. Do not break yarn.

**Right front:**
Row 1: Right side of work. Draw through 26 lps (13 patts across). Turn.
Row 2: As row 2.
Rep. last 2 rows from armhole until 6 patts length have been worked. Fasten off.

**Neck:**
Row 1: Leave 6 patts across, join to next patt. Draw through 14 lps.
Row 2: As row 2. Fasten off.

**Back:**
Right side of work, leave 3 patts for armhole, join to next patt. Draw through 54 lps.
Work patt, until 7 patts length have been worked from armhole. Fasten off.

**Left front:**
Row 1: Right side of work, leave 3 patts for armhole, join to next patt. Draw through 26 lps ending to front edge. Turn.
Row 2: As row 2.
Rep. last 2 rows from armhole until 6 patts length have been worked ending at armhole.
Row 1: Draw through 14 lps, leave 6 patts for neck. Turn.
Row 2: As row 2. Fasten off.
Join shoulders.

**Borders**
Wrong side of work, left bottom edge, 1 dc evenly, not loosely, left side to neck, rnd neck, then right side. Fasten off.

**Neck:** wrong side, left front corner, dc to right corner front. Fasten off. Rep as last row once more rnd neck. Fasten off.

**Armholes:** wrong side of work, dc rnd not loose, ss to 1st dc. Fasten off.

*Icelandic coat*

# Icelandic coat

**Sample**
With 25 mm Whizz Pin and 7.00 hook, make 21 ch. (See pp. 4–5).
Row 1: 1 dc into 2nd ch from hook, 1 dc into each ch st to end of row (20 dc).
Row 2: 2ch, 1 hlf tr into each dc. (20 hlf tr).
Row 3: 1 ch, 1 dc into each hlf tr. (20 dc).
Row 4: Draw through 20 lps.
Row 5: 5 dc into 5 lps tog. Rep to end of row. (4 patts across).
Row 6: As row 2.
Row 7: As row 3.
Last 4 rows form patt.

**Size:** Bust 91/96 cm (36/38 in). Length from back of neck 81 cm (32 in). Sleeve length 43 cm (17 in).

**Tension:** 2 patts – 8 cm (3 in) across.

**Materials:** 10 (100 grm) balls Icelandic Samband Lopi. 1 25 mm (1 in) Whizz Pin. 7.00 and 6.00 crochet hooks.
With 7.00 hook make 131 ch.
Row 1: 1 dc into 2nd ch from hook, 1 dc into each ch to end of row. (130 dc).
Row 2: 2 ch, 1 hlf tr into each dc. (130 hlf tr).
Row 3: 1 ch, 1 dc into each half tr. (130 dc).
Row 4: Draw through 130 lps.
Row 5: 5 dc into 5 lps tog. Rep to end of row (26 patts across).
Row 6: As row 2.
Row 7: As row 3.
Last 4 rows form patt.
Rep last 4 rows until 9 patts length have been worked, then work rows 4, 5 and 6, shape front, 1 ch, 1 dc into each hlf tr 25 times. Turn.

**Right front:**
Row 1: Draw through 25 lps. Turn.
Row 2: 5 dc into 5 lps tog. 5 times. (5 patts across). Turn.

# Icelandic 'V' neck sweater

**Sample**
With 20 mm Whizz Pin and 5.00 hook, make 20 ch. (See pp. 4–5).
Row 1: Draw through 20 lps, on to Whizz Pin.
Row 2: 4 dc into 4 lps tog. Rep to end of row. (5 patts across).
Last 2 rows form patt.

**Size:** Bust 81/86 cm (32/34 in). Length of sleeve 46 cm (18 in). Length from back of neck 63 cm (25 in).

**Tension:** 2 patts – 5 cm (2 in) across.

**Materials:** 7 (50 grm) balls Icelandic Samband Saga. 1 20 mm (¾ in) Whizz Pin. 4.00 and 5.00 crochet hooks.

**Back:** With 5.00 hook make 73 ch.
Row 1: 1 dc into 2nd ch from hook, 1 dc into each ch, to end of row (72 dc).
Row 2: Draw through 72 lps.
Row 3: 4 dc into 4 lps tog. Rep to end of row. (18 patts across).
**Rep last 2 rows 22 times. Fasten off.

**Front:** Work exactly as back until ** Rep patt 14 times length ending on dc row.

**Shape neck:**
Row 1: Draw through 36 lps (9 patts across) leaving 9 patts turn.
Row 2: 2 dc into 4 lps tog * (4 dc into 4 lps tog) rep from * to end of row.

*Icelandic 'V'-neck sweater*

Row 3: 2 ch, 1 hlf tr into each dc. 25 times. Turn.
Row 4: 1 ch, 1 dc into each half tr. 25 times. Turn.
Rep last 4 rows until 3 patts length from armhole.
Shape neck:
Row 1: Draw through 20 lps. Turn.
Row 2: 5 dc into 5 lps tog. 4 times. (4 patts across).
Row 3: 2 ch, 1 hlf tr into each dc. (20 hlf tr).
Row 4: 1 ch, 1 dc into each half tr. Fasten off.

**Left front:**
**Right Side:** Join wool 5 patts from armhole, 1 ch. (1 dc into each hlf tr) 25 times. Turn.
Row 1: Draw through 25 lps.
Row 2: 5 dc into 5 lps tog. 5 times. (5 patts across).
Row 3: 2 ch, 1 half tr into each dc. 25 times.
Row 4: 1 ch, 1 dc into each half tr. 25 times.
Rep last 4 rows until 3 patts length from armhole. Fasten off.

**Shape neck:**
Wrong Side, front edge, miss 1 patt, join wool.
Row 1: Draw through 20 lps.
Row 2: 5 dc into 5 lps tog. 4 times. (4 patts across).
Row 3: 2 ch, 1 hlf tr into each dc. (20 hlf tr).
Row 4: 1 ch, 1 dc into each hlf tr. (20 dc). Fasten off.

**Back:**
Right side, work across 12 patts, leaving 2 patts each side for armholes. 1 ch 1 dc into each hlf tr. (60 dc).
Work 4 patts length from armholes. Fasten off.

**Sleeves:**
Make 51 ch.
Row 1: 1 dc into 2nd ch from hook, 1 dc into each ch. (50 dc).
Row 2: 2 ch, 1 hlf tr into each dc. (50 hlf tr).
Row 3: 1 ch, 1 dc into each hlf tr. (50 dc).
Row 4: Draw through 50 lps.
Row 5: 5 dc into 5 lps tog rep to end of row. (10 patts across).
Row 6: As row 2.
Row 7: As row 3.
Rep last 4 rows until 7 patts length have been worked. Fasten off. Sew shoulder seams.

**Border:**
**Left front edge:**
Row 1: With 7.00 hook, join from neck *(6 dc between patt) rep from * to bottom edge, ending 3 dc. (81 dc). Turn.
Row 2: With 6.00 hook, 2 ch, 1 hlf tr into each dc. (81 hlf tr). Turn.
Row 3: 1 ch miss 1 hlf tr 1 dc into each hlf tr. (80 dc). Turn.
Row 4: Draw through 80 lps.
Row 5: 5 dc into 5 lps tog. (16 patts across).
Row 6: As row 2.
Row 7: 1 ch, 1 dc into each hlf tr. Fasten off.

**Right front edge:** Work to match left front then neck border.
With 7.00 hook 60 dc rnd neck. Turn.
With 6.00 hook, work border as front edge, then 8 dc into 4 border edges.

**Armhole edge.** With 7.00 hook, 1 dc into each hlf tr, 6 dc between each patt.
Sew in sleeves.

**Acknowledgements**

Text and patterns by Margaret Helen Wilks

First published in 1986
by Search Press Limited
Wellwood, North Farm Road
Tunbridge Wells,
Kent TN2 3DR

in association with
W.I. Books Ltd
39 Eccleston Street
Victoria
London
SW1W 9NT



The author would like to thank Pam Harper for testing the patterns



Search Press ISBN 0 85532 591 7
W.I. Books ISBN 0 947990 20 8

Typeset by Phoenix Photosetting, Chatham
Made and printed in Spain by A.G.Elkar S.Coop. Bilbao-12

# Mohair top

**Sample**
Note: dc row is the wrong side of work. 2 balls are worked tog.
With 25 mm Whizz Pin and 7.00 hook, 2 balls, make 15 ch. (See pp. 4–5).
Row 1: Draw lps through ch sts on to Whizz Pin. (15 lps).
Row 2: 3 dc into 3 lps tog. Rep to end of row.
Row 3: Draw through 15 lps.
Row 4: 3 dc into 3 lps tog. Rep to end of row.
Last 2 rows form patt.

**Size:** Bust 86/91 cm (34/36 in). **Length:** from shoulder 63½ cm (25 in).

**Tension:** 2 patts – 6 cm (2¼ in) across, (using two strands tog, 3 dc into 3 lps tog).

**Materials:** 14 (25 grm) balls Emu Butterfly, 1 25 mm (1 in) Whizz Pin, 6.00 and 7.00 crochet hooks.

Note: Work with 2 strands tog.

**Front and back alike:**
**Left shoulder:** With 7.00 hook 2 strands tog make 12 ch.
Row 1: Draw through 12 lps (right side of work).
Row 2: 3 dc into 3 lps tog, rep to end of row. (4 patts across).
Rep last 2 rows twice more, last row continue to make 24 ch for neck. Leave for right shoulder, do not break yarn. With 7.00 hook make 12 ch.
Row 1: Draw through 12 lps.
Row 2: 3 dc into 3 lps tog, rep to end of row. (4 patts across).
Rep last 2 rows once then row 1, break yarn, join ch to lps, 3 dc into 3 lps tog across 4 patts.

Row 1: Draw through 12 lps. Neck 24 lps, into each ch st. then 12 lps (48 lps).
Row 2: 3 dc into 3 lps tog, rep to end of row. (16 patts across).
Row 3: Draw through 48 lps.
Row 4: As row 2.
Rep last 2 rows until 10 patts length have been worked from shoulder.

**Waist:**
Row 1: Draw through 48 lps.
Row 2: 2 dc into 2 lps tog, rep to end of row.
Rep last 2 rows until 6 patts length from waist have been worked. Fasten off.

**Making up:**
Sew shoulders tog, side seams leaving 5 patts back and front for armholes.

**Border:**
Right side, with 6.00 hook, join to back of neck *(1 dc into each ch st) twice, miss 1 ch, rep from * to side of shoulder, 3 dc into each patt to front, work front of neck as back, then shoulder as other side to the beg. ss to join. Fasten off.